BASIC TRAINING

The 7 Essentials for Spiritual Maturity

Vanable H Moody II

Introduction

The following outlines are the products of a desire to produce the fruit of spiritual maturity and reproduction in the lives of faithful believers. Effective ministry is not possible without it.

God has called pastor/teachers to prepare believers for ministry. As long as pastors treat the task of preparing the church for ministry as secondary, the Great Commission will go unfulfilled and the body of Christ will be one-dimensional. God has called the whole Church to ministry, not just the apostles, prophets, evangelists, pastors and teachers, but the whole Church! According to the Word of God, the primary responsibility of the Pastor is to teach and to prepare the people to minister to the world. (Ephesians 4:11-12)

It's important that we begin with this biblical understanding because contemporarily, many churches don't follow this mandate. Whether it is because of buying into a Messiah Complex or collapsing under historical and cultural expectations, much of the failure of the people of God to minister is due, in large measure, to the failure of pastors to effectively teach and prepare them. This book is my attempt to help correct this problem in the local church. The inspiration for this book belongs to Gilbert Thompson. His book, <u>Introduction to Foundations</u>, which is now out of print, transformed my life and helped me to understand the significance of this type of study for believers.

There are seven areas that are essential for spiritual maturity: Christ, Word, Prayer, Fellowship, Followship, Stewardship and Ministry. Christ is the central area; the other six are connected to Him. Three of the areas, Word, Prayer, and Stewardship deal with our vertical relationship with God. The other three remaining areas, Fellowship, Followship, and Ministry, deal with our horizontal relationship with our fellow man.

I named them, *"The Seven Essentials for Spiritual Maturity,"* because of the spiritual progression of each level. To each level, I attached a confession and a word following each confession, indicating the active spiritual position of the believer. For example, when you are grounded in the First Essential, Christ, you will be able to confess, "I am in faith." The word, "standing," refers to your spiritual position in Christ; you are standing in Christ by faith. Therefore, you would say, "I am in faith - standing." Or, if you were talking about being grounded in the Second Essential, Word, you would be able to say, "I am in obedience - walking," and so forth.

Each of the seven essentials has three outlines, totaling twenty-one outlines when combined. The outlines are numbered in succession, one through twenty-one. Also included in this foundational study are Scriptures to be memorized (references and verses). Notice that the verses under each level deal with the truth of that level. Finally, following each of the seven essentials is a page of study questions. Use it to test your retention of the truth in the section. Remember, it is by the faithful study of the Word that the believer is approved. (2 Timothy 2:15)

May you "Grow in the grace and knowledge of our Lord and Savior Jesus Christ. To Him be glory both now and forever. Amen." (2 Peter 3:18)

Outline: Seven Essentials for Spiritual Maturity

Memory Scriptures

Scriptures to be memorized with each section: 42
Scriptures total: 6 in each section.

1. Christ
2 Corinthians 5:17   Hebrews 11:6   John 15:5
Acts 17:30-31   John 5:24   Hebrews 6:1-2

2. Word
Matthew 4:4   Psalm 119:9-11   John 14:21
2 Timothy 3:16   Colossians 3:16   I Peter 1:23

3. Prayer
John 16:24   Psalm 16:11   I John 5:14-15
I John 1:9   Philippians 4:6-7   Ephesians 6:18

4. Fellowship
Acts 2:42-44   Titus 2:12-13   2 Corinthians 1:3-4
I John 1:7   Hebrews 10:25   Galatians 5:22-23

5. Followship
1 Corinthians 14:40	Psalm 133	Acts 2:42-43
Exodus 17:8-13	1 Samuel 8:6-9	Hebrews 4:14-16

6. Stewardship
Deuteronomy 10:14	Matthew 25:21	2 Corinthians 9:6-8
Malachi 3:8-12	Matthew 2:11	1 Corinthians 13:3

7. Ministry
Romans 3:23	Acts 1:8	John 1:12
Romans 10:9-10	Romans 5:8	Luke 9:23

Essential One
Christ

This first essential of spiritual maturity, Christ, is the beginning because Jesus Christ is the ultimate Foundation Stone. In this section, we will look at the person of Jesus Christ, His work and how we make Him Lord of our lives.

First, we ask the Christological question, "Who is Jesus?" The answers to all of our spiritual questions are found in the Scriptures. As we let the Scriptures speak to us, we begin to realize experientially, the power of the words of God. God has spoken to us through the writings of godly men who were influenced by the Holy Spirit (2 Peter 1:21). By hearing and obeying the Scriptures, we train ourselves in righteousness (2 Timothy 3:16). By understanding what the Scriptures teach about the person of Jesus, we add increase to our lives. Through that increase comes faith (Romans 10:17), peace (Romans 5:1), and new life in His name (John 20:31). The goal of this first level is to ground the new believer in Christ so that he can confess with assurance, "I am in faith - standing."

Second, we ask the Soteriological question, "What did Jesus do?" What did Jesus accomplish during His first coming, over 2000 years ago, in His incarnation? The answer is that Jesus accomplishes two foundational things during His first coming and they are connected. First, He purchased eternal salvation by the shedding of His blood on the cross at Calvary (John 3:16; Acts 20:28), and second, He established His Church (Matthew 16:13-21). Jesus made disciples by teaching and training men and women during His earthly ministry. Accordingly, His disciples knew who He was, the Christ, the Son of the living God (Matthew 16:16), and eventually, they understood what He came to earth to do.

Third, we ask the important practical question, "How do I make Jesus Lord?" Everyone should understand that by confessing Jesus as Lord, believing that He has risen from the dead and by being baptized in water, you are saved in the act of a moment. But to establish the lordship of Christ in your life as a lifestyle requires more. It is a process. This outline deals with that process by telling us what we must do. The key passage in this process is Hebrews 6:1-2, the elementary teachings about Christ: repentance, faith, baptisms, laying on of hands, resurrection and judgment. The understanding and practice of these elementary teachings will establish and anchor the new believer, giving him a solid foundation. The ultimate goal of this level is to ground the new believer in Christ so that he is able to confess, "I am in faith

- standing." This primary assurance is both basic and necessary.

The confession: I am in Faith - Standing.

Areas covered in this section:

1. Christology: Who is Jesus of Nazareth?
2. Soteriology: What did Jesus do during His first advent?
3. Application: How do I make Jesus Lord?

Outline 1. Christology: Who is Jesus of Nazareth?

"Who is Jesus of Nazareth?" is the most important question, historical or otherwise, that anyone can ask. To know who Jesus is, means to know the way to salvation (John 14:6), the door to abundant life (John 10:1-10), and the truth that makes men free (John 8:31-32). In this brief space, we will take a fundamental glimpse at the person named Jesus of Nazareth. We will examine, by scriptural references, some of the titles and offices of Jesus.

A. Lord. The word Lord, as it is applied to Jesus of Nazareth, means that this One is the eternal God manifested in the flesh. He was called Lord at His birth (Luke 2:11); He is proclaimed Lord by His resurrection (Acts 2:36); acknowledging His lordship is a prerequisite for salvation (Romans 10:9); and the apostles taught that Jesus emptied Himself of equality with God and that God exalted Him to the position where, one day, every knee shall bow and every tongue shall confess that Jesus is Lord (Philippians 2:5-11).

B. Messiah. When Jesus asked his disciples who they thought he was (Matthew 16:13-20), Peter answered, "You are the Christ, the Son of the living God." The New Testament word Christ is a Greek word, which means "the anointed one" (the Old Testament word Messiah is the Hebrew word which means "the anointed one"). Jesus praised Peter for answering the questions correctly. Jesus is the Christ, the Messiah and the Anointed One from God. In prophetic terms, He is the fulfillment of the Old Testament Messianic promises to the children of Israel (Genesis 3:15; 49:10-11; Numbers 24:17, 19: Deuteronomy 18:15, 18; 2 Samuel 7:12-13; Psalm 2:2; 100:1,4; Isaiah 7:15, 9:6-7, 53; Jeremiah 23:5-6). Included in each of these Old Testament prophecies of the Jewish Messiah is a clear reference to the coming of One anointed by God to fulfill a specific mission. All of these prophecies find their ultimate and highest fulfillment in one person in history-Jesus of Nazareth.

C. Prophet. By definition, a prophet is one who speaks for God to men. Jesus, during His earthly ministry, delivered the living Word of God to His generation. He preached, taught, and spoke in parables (human stories that illustrate spiritual truth). He discipled men. Moses predicted that the Messiah would be a prophet (Deuteronomy 18:15); Stephen confirmed that this was fulfilled in Jesus (Acts 7:37); Jesus called Himself a prophet (Matthew 13:57); the people called Him a prophet (Matthew 21:11); and today, Jesus continues to fulfill the ministry of a prophet, one who speaks for God (Hebrews1:1-2).

D. Priest. A priest is one who represents the people to God; one who speaks to God for the people. Jesus is our faithful high priest who represented us on the cross (Hebrews 2:17-18; 7:26-27); He is our great high priest who is in the presence of God (Hebrews 4:14-16) interceding for us (Romans 8:34; Hebrews 7:25).

E. King. Jesus of Nazareth being a king means that He is in the lineage of King David (Matthew 1:6; Luke 3:31). The Messiah was to be a son of David (Matthew 1:1; 22:41-42). Further, Jesus is king means that the Messianic Kingdom Age is now (Zechariah 9:9; Matthew 21:5-9; John 1:19: 18:37), and that He will be the king who returns (Matthew 25:34; Revelation 19:16).

Conclusion: Jesus of Nazareth was both God and man.

Notes

He came to earth to
save man from destruction
(from himself)

Outline 2. Soteriology: What did Jesus do during His first advent?
(appearing)

What did Jesus do? This is an important historical question because it deals with the eternal purpose of God for mankind. Using the Scriptures as our source for information, we will take a brief, yet basic look into the two major accomplishments of Christ during His first advent. The word "advent" means "appearing." The "first advent" or "first appearing" of Jesus was that time, over 2000 years ago, when Jesus came to earth, was born of the virgin Mary, lived approximately 33 years, and was crucified on the cross by Roman soldiers. Therefore, what did Jesus accomplish during his first advent?

A. The Atonement.

   1. Jesus was the Lamb of God sent to take away the sins of the world. (John 1:29)

   2. Jesus' death on the cross demonstrates the love of God for the entire world. (John 3:16; Romans 5:8)

   3. Jesus purchased eternal salvation by the shedding of His blood on the cross at Calvary. (Acts 20:28; 1 Peter 1:18-19)

B. The establishment of the Church.

A body of believers

1. Jesus called and taught disciples. (Matthew 4:18-20; 5:1-2)

2. Jesus gave His disciples authority and power to minister in His name. (Matthew 10:1; Luke 10:19; Matthew 28:18-19; Acts 1:8)

3. Jesus established His Church upon Himself, meaning that He was the Christ, the Son of the living God (Matthew 16:13-21); upon His death on the cross and resurrection, the atonement (1 Corinthians 15:1-4; Acts 20:28); and upon the apostles and prophets. (Ephesians 2:20)

Notes

Outline 3. Application: How do I make Jesus Lord?

No one can make Jesus Lord without doing what the Bible says. In the elementary teachings about Christ found in Hebrews 6:1-2, the writer outlines all that the new believer needs to do to make Jesus Lord. Following these teachings will establish the new believer foundationally. It is important to understand them fully because of their instructional value in leading the new believer into a personal relationship with God through Christ.

Six elementary teachings about Christ are listed in Hebrews 6:1-2. A clear understanding of each leads to being grounded in the lordship of Jesus Christ.

> *Therefore let us leave the elementary teachings about Christ and go on to maturity, not laying again the foundation of* **repentance** *from acts that lead to death, and of* **faith** *in God, instruction about* **baptisms**, *the* **laying on of hands**, *the* **resurrection** *of the dead, and the eternal* **judgment**. *(Hebrews 6:1-2)*

Notice that I have highlighted the six elementary teachings about Christ in the above passage. Remember, understanding each teaching is fundamental to being grounded in Christ. These six teachings are important.

A. **Repentance.** This is a change of mind ("metanoia" in the Greek) often accompanied by a feeling of regret or remorse ("nâcham" in the Hebrew); in short – a turning away from sin to God ("shûwb" in the Hebrew). These are the literal meanings of the Greek and Hebrew words that are most often translated by the English word "repent." Walking in the Lordship of Christ means walking in repentance. Repentance moves from being just an act of the past to being a lifestyle of the present. The new believer begins to operate with a "changed mind." His mind is renewed (Romans 12:2; Ephesians 4:23) and his actions reflect the reality of a new creation (2 Corinthians 5:17; Ephesians 4:24). The key is that repentance is practiced as a part of a daily attitude, one where repentance is not negative but positive; where change means growth and development. Change is good and repentance is of God.

Repentance Scriptures: Matthew 21:29-31; Luke 15:11-31; 2 Corinthians 7:10

B.   Faith. By definition, it is believing that you have what God's Word says you have in spite of the fact that you do not yet see it or feel it. To be grounded in the lordship of Christ and using the elementary teaching of faith is to have the assurance of salvation. The new believer knows that he has the right to call himself a child of God because he has received Christ by faith and has believed in

Psalm 139

He gives us Wisdom, it only comes from him.

Lord not my will, but yours.

Lord show me your will.

* Be anxious for nothing, but everything
in prayer + supplication + thanksgiving.

Phil 4:6

His name (John 1:12). Faith believes that God
has done what He promised, and rejoices.
Faith understands that God cannot lie, and
therefore, stands anchored in the trustworthy
nature of God's unchanging promises.

Faith scriptures: Romans 4:17; 10:8-10;
Hebrews 11:1, 6.

C. Baptisms. Before the new believer can be
grounded in the Lordship of Christ through
the elementary teaching about baptisms, he
must understand the meaning of baptism.

1. The baptism (immersion) of believers in
water, by a minister, in the name of the
Lord is called Christian Baptism or Water
Baptism (Matthew 28:19; Acts 2:38;
Romans 6:3-9; Colossians 2:12).

There is some controversy over baptismal
formula - the words that are stated over the candi-
date by the believer baptizing him. There are those
who use the Trinitarian formula given by Jesus in
Matthew 28:19, and others who insist that baptism
is not genuine unless it is done "in the name of the
Lord Jesus Christ" (Acts 2:38). The truth is that all
water baptism should be performed "in the name of
the Lord Jesus Christ," meaning that all should know
that it is by the authority of the words of Jesus that
we baptize believers.

Years ago, according to my scriptural understanding of the truth of water baptism, I wrote the following formula:

> *(Name of candidate, upon the profession of your faith, and your belief in our Lord and Savior Jesus the Christ, I now baptize you in the name of the Father, and of the Son, and of the Holy Spirit.)*

This formula satisfies the issues of both sides of the controversy and should not be offensive to either.

D. The laying on of hands. This is the scriptural practice where the mature believer places his hands on another believer for the purpose of imparting spiritual blessing. As a part of the elementary teachings about Christ, the laying on of hands means submission to the authority of leaders within the local church. The spiritual benefits are in one or more of the following areas:

1. Blessing: Genesis 48:13-20; Mark 10:13-16

2. Healing: Mark 6:5; 16:18; Luke 4:40; 13:13; Acts 28:8

3. Anointing, Ordination: Acts 6:6; 13:3: 1 Timothy 4:14; 2 Timothy 1:6

E. Resurrection. This part of the elementary teachings about Christ deal with the new life the new believer receives through exercising faith in the resurrected Christ. He is born again, and therefore experiences spiritual resurrection (John 5:24-25; Ephesians 2:1, King James Version (KJV)). The new birth is a spiritual resurrection from being dead in trespasses and sins, to becoming a new creation in Christ (2 Corinthians 5:17). Resurrection speaks of God's grace experienced through faith in the resurrection of Christ, which provides access for us to experience new life (Romans 5:2).

Also, resurrection deals with the general resurrection of the dead, which will take place at the last day when Jesus Christ comes again (John 6:39, 40, 44, 54; 11:24).

Resurrection Scriptures
- Resurrection of Christ: 1 Corinthians 15
- Spiritual resurrection: John 5:24-25; Ephesians 2:1, KJV
- General resurrection of the dead: Daniel 12:2; John 5:28-29; Acts 24:15

F. Judgment. In this part of the elementary teachings about Christ, the new believer recognizes that he has been judged (past), is being judged (present), and will be judged (future). The exhortation to the new believer is to "walk circumspectly"- being very careful how he lives (Ephesians 5:15-16, KJV and NIV), knowing that he will be judged according to the deeds performed in his body (2 Corinthians 5:10).

This should not create condemnation (Romans 8:1) but sober thinking (Romans 12:3), which will lead the convert to focus on godly character (Titus 2:12, KJV) in his daily walk.

Judgment Scriptures:
- Past, the convicting ministry of the Holy Spirit, which leads us to be a believer: John 16:8-11
- Present, the preliminary judgment ministry of the Word of God to us: James 1:25; I John 1:7; I Peter 4:17. In this regard, when we partake of the Lord's Supper, it should be a time when we examine ourselves as members of the covenant community. Maintaining reconciled relations with our brethren is a part of "recognizing the body of the Lord" (I Corinthians 11:28-29).
- Future, the final judgment and rewarding of the saved according to their work: I Corinthians 3:6-15; 2 Corinthians 5:10.

Notes

Study Questions: Essential One

1. What is the First Essential of Spiritual Maturity?

   Christ

2. What is the confession that a believer can make after being grounded in the First Essential?

   I am in Faith s

3. What are the five titles that we use to teach who Jesus is?

   Lord

   Messiah

   Prophet

   Priest

   King

4. What are the Hebrew and Greek words that mean "the anointed one?"

   Christ & Messiah

5. Jesus came as the Lamb of God to... (John 1:29)

   To take away the sins

6. The "first advent" is the

   appearing

7. What body did Jesus establish through discipleship?

_____*Church*_____

_____

8. What are the six elementary teachings about Christ? (Hebrews 6:1-2)

Repent

Faith

Baptism

Laying of Hands

Faith

Judgement

The word of God is essential
I can be obedient if I stay
in the word of God. Walk
in the word. Study thing

Essential Two
Word

This second essential for spiritual maturity, "Word," focuses on laying a foundation through obeying what God has said in His word. There can be no adequate treatment of Christ, nor of the salvation He offers, without the Word. The phrases - the Word, the Bible, and the Holy Scriptures all refer to the same sacred writings.

The first outline (Outline 4) asks the question, "What are the evidences of the trustworthiness of the Bible?" By teaching the biblical Doctrine of Inspiration, this outline will deal with the internal and external evidences, which support the truth that the bible "IS" the Word of God. In this day of the liberal and neo-orthodox attacks on the trustworthiness of the Bible, this basic teaching is much needed.

The internal evidences are those evidences that come from within the Scriptures themselves. What does the Bible say about itself? What did the writers of the Bible say about themselves? What about the unity of the Bible? What did Jesus believe about the trustworthiness of the scriptures? All of these questions and other issues are briefly dealt with in this first outline.

The external evidences are those evidences that come from outside the Scriptures themselves. Evidences such as the effects of the Scriptures on human history and the existence of the Church, make up the substance of the teaching in this outline.

The second outline (Outline 5) deals with the practical, obedient use of the Scriptures in the everyday life of the believer. It will answer the question, "How and where do I begin in my study of the Bible?" Our goal is to briefly describe the basic tools and how – to's of establishing a fruitful devotional life. There are many names given to this daily Christian discipline. One of the popular names is "quiet time." Most Christians fail in this basic spiritual discipline. This session will help the new convert by emphasizing easy practical steps. Following these steps will help him or her establish a strong devotional habit, which will anchor his or her life. The metaphorical picture of the confession, "I am in obedience-walking," refers to the believer's foundation-laying walk of obedience and it is also the goal of this section. Jesus taught us that the foundation of obedience will fortify our lives against all storms. (Matthew 7:24-25)

The third outline (Outline 6) asks the questions, "Who am I? What do I have? And what can I do?" Understanding the benefits of a good confession is one of the goals of this outline. A good confession is a confession based upon faith in the Word. To "confess" literally means, "to say the same thing." The promises of the Word of God actually begin to influence what we think, believe and speak. Genuine faith is established through this (Romans 10:17) and prosperity in your circumstances follows. Understanding what faith is and how it works is a part of the strategy behind this outline. Since faith comes by hearing the Word of God (Romans 10:17), encouraging the new believer to speak the Word will be a faith building discipline.

The confession: I am in Obedience - Walking.

Areas covered in this section:

4. What are the evidences of the trustworthiness of the Bible?
5. How and where do I begin?
6. Who am I, what do I have, and what can I do?

Outline 4. What are the evidences of the trustworthiness of the Bible?

The Bible is the revealed Word of God. The Bible does not contain the Word of God as some liberal theologians say. Nor does the Bible become the Word of God as some neo-orthodox theologians say. The Bible is the Word of God from Genesis to Revelation. The Bible is a unique book. It is holy writ. There is no other collection of writings in all of history that equals the holiness, the authority, and the impact upon humankind, as that of the Bible. As the Word of God, the following is true; the Bible is:

- **Alive:** It is a living seed, producing faith and fruit. (Luke 8:11; Hebrews 4:12; Romans 10:17)

- **Food:** It is nourishment for your spirit. (1 Peter 2:2; Matthew 4:4; Jeremiah 15:16)

- **Authority:** It does not change; there is none higher. (Psalm 119; 89)

- **Powerful:** It can transform. (Romans 1:16)

- **Spiritual:** It is truth from the realm of God. (John 6:63)

A. Internal Evidence - Evidence from the writings themselves.

1. New Testament writers, Paul and Peter, called the Scriptures the inspired Word of God. (2 Timothy 3:16; 2 Peter 1:21)

2. The Apostle Peter equated the writings of Paul with Scripture. (2 Peter 3:15-16)

3. In the Old Testament alone, there are over 2000 phrases such as, "And God spoke to Moses," "the word of the Lord came unto," and "God said." The Bible is the

record of the works and deeds of God in history.

4. The unity of the Bible points to the supernatural guidance of the Almighty. The Bible was written over a period of about 1500 years (15 centuries!), by more than 40 different writers from a variety of backgrounds, living on three different continents, in three different languages (Hebrew, Greek, and Aramaic), and yet there is a oneness, a unity, within the book. (It is sometimes difficult to get even two or three people to agree, much less 40 individuals from different cultures and from different periods of time!) The Bible deals with many controversial subjects, yet there is one theme: the Bible is about Jesus, the Messiah.

5. Jesus said that the Scriptures testified of Him (John 5:39, 46, 47). He used the Scriptures to explain who He was (Luke 24:27, 44). The book is about Jesus from cover to cover. The Old Testament is the preparation (Isaiah 40:3). The Gospels are the manifestation (John 1:29). The Book of Acts is the propagation (Acts 1:8). The Epistles give the explanation (Colossians 1:27). The Revelation is the consummation (Revelation 1:7).

6. Jesus believed the Scriptures to be the inspired Word of God (Matthew 5:17-18; John 10:35). He also said that His word would not pass away (Matthew 24:35).

B. External Evidence - Evidence outside of the writings themselves:

1. The existence and testimony of the early church: There is no way to explain the existence and survival of the early church apart from the truth of the historical accounts of the resurrection of Christ.

2. The witness of history and archaeology: No archaeological find has ever shown the Scriptures to be historically inaccurate. In fact, archaeology has again and again proved the historical accuracy of the Scriptures.

3. The supernatural influence of the Scriptures upon the lives of people down through the centuries

Notes

Outline 5. How and where do I begin?

Before we begin to answer the above question, there are three important things that the new believer must have in order to fully understand and benefit from the wisdom of this spiritual book referred to as the Bible:

A. The Holy Spirit: The apostle Paul wrote to the Corinthians,

> *However, as it is written: "No eye has seen, no ear has heard, no mind has conceived what God has prepared for those who love Him"- but God has revealed it to us by His Spirit. The Spirit searches all things, even the deep things of God. (I Corinthians 2:9-10)*

The new believer needs to be filled with the Holy Spirit (Ephesians 5:18) so that He can guide him into all truth (John 16:13). Even beginners can pray and ask the Holy Spirit to open their eyes to the truth of the Word (Psalm 119:18).

B. The willingness to obey: If anyone obeys it, this spiritual book holds the potential of great benefit for them. No one can benefit from its promises if they do not meet its conditions. Remember, God's promises are never without the condition of obedience. The apostle James said,

3 things I need 1) Holy Spirit (invite him in)

Do not merely listen to the Word, and so deceive yourselves. Do what it says. (James 1:22)

C. **A plan:** Simply stated, the plan for the new believer is getting into the Word of God and letting the Word of God get into him. There are three basic hermeneutical or Bible-understanding tools that the beginner should consistently use to help him in his studying, observation, interpretation and application.

- Observation - taking note of all that is there in the passage

- Interpretation - understanding what the passage meant to the writer and the addresses by analyzing the meanings of the words, the grammar, the history and the context

- Application- allowing the truth of the passage to affect your experience through the discipline of obedience

How and where do you begin this obedience training?

The new believer should:

    1. Begin by establishing a time and a place for the devotional reading of the Word of God. Be consistent. It is better to

consistently study the Word for 5 minutes a day than to haphazardly read it an hour every other week.

2. Ask for the guidance of the Holy Spirit (John 16:13; Psalm 119:18). Spend time in praise and worship before you read the Word.

3. Read the New Testament first.

    a. Read the Gospels in this order: Mark, Matthew, John, and Luke/Acts (these two works by the same author should be read together). These deal with the life of Jesus and the early Church.

    b. Read the epistles. You should stay in one book until you finish reading it. You should underline verses that especially minister to you and start to memorize them.

4. Read the Psalms and Proverbs daily. There is merit in the devotional reading of the Proverbs in the mornings for their wisdom and the Psalms in the evenings for their encouragement. (See Appendix A)

5. Read the Old Testament history, the books from Genesis to Esther. The prophets should be read along with a guide to help explain the historical period of the writer. I recommend- *Survey of the Old Testament Introduction* by Gleason Archer.

6. Read the Revelation (and other apocalyptic literature) only after you have a thorough knowledge of the Old and New Testaments.

✳ 7. Memorize the Word topics (Psalm 119:11; 2 Timothy 2:15; I Peter 3:15). After completing the memorization of the scriptures in this book (See Scripture Memory, page 5), you should purchase the Topical Memory System (TMS) by Navigators.
Meditate (means "chew the cud", repeat slowly to himself and reflect) upon the rich truths received from the Word (Joshua 1:8; Psalm 1:2). Meditation is closely linked with memorization and application.

8. Get into the habit of listening to spiritual music or tapes about the Word throughout the day or whenever possible. This will assist you in constantly making melody in your heart unto the Lord (Ephesians

5:19; Colossians 3:16) and it will keep your mind upon the things of God (Isaiah 26:3). Plan times of prayer and praise throughout the day. Do not leave it to chance. Remember Daniel - he planned to pray three times a day. He established an excellent habit, and he reaped great benefit from it. The new believer should do likewise.

Conclusion: Bear in mind that there is no substitute for time. The consistent faithful practice of the above will bring results as the new believer takes the time to meditate (repeat slowly to himself) upon what he is reading and learning, and carefully applies the truths learned to his life. All should be encouraged to take time to wait reverently in the Lord's presence for the wisdom of His insight. The solid foundation, that all of us need, begins to be established in us when we submit to Christ. It further develops as we consistently obey the Word of God. Let's remember that the key ingredient for foundational development is obedience. Jesus taught:

> *Therefore everyone who hears these words of mine and puts them into practice is like a wise man who built his house on the rock. The rain came down, the streams rose, and the winds blew and beat against that house; yet it did not fall, because it had its foundation on the rock. But everyone who hears these words of mine and does not put*

them into practice is like a foolish man who builds his house on sand. The rain came down, the streams rose, and the winds blew and beat against that house and it fell with a great crash. (Matthew 7:24-27)

The key is obedience, obedience, obedience!

Notes

Who I am in Christ?

- I'm blessed + highly favored
- I'm a child of God
- I'm a new creation
- I'm redeemed
- I'm righteous
- I'm covered (Jesus, thank you)
- I'm shielded
-

What do I have in Christ?

I have abundant life   (Gal
I have the fruit of the spirit 5:22
I have authority (give gave it to
me!
I have access to Christ (anytime - anywhere

What can I do in Christ?

- Walk in Victory
- Understand the Word
- Pray c Confidence
- Be faithful
- Witness c Power
- Fellowship

Outline 6. Who am I, what do I have, and what can I do?

What does it mean to make a good confession? Making a good confession is making a confession based upon faith in the Word of God. The word "confess" literally means, "to say the same thing." In making a good confession, the new believer says the same thing about himself that God says about him. If God says, "I have blessed you," he says, "I am blessed." He agrees with God. He believes what God says about **who he is, what he has, and what he can do.** After repentance and faith (Acts 20:21), he confesses that Jesus is Lord (Romans 10:9), believes that he is saved by faith and confirms that faith through obeying the command to be baptized (Acts 2:38). He then boldly confesses **who he is** in Christ, based upon his faith in the authority of the promises of the Word and his obedience to them. Knowing and confessing **what he has** and **what he can do** is also based upon his understanding of the truth and authority of the promises of the Word and his obedience to them.

The goal of this session is to establish the truth of scriptural confession in the life of the new believer. He must learn to believe and then confess, by faith, who he is in Christ (according to redemption promises), what he has in Christ (according to His provision promises), what he can do in Christ (according to His enablement promises). He must learn to say about himself what God says about him, in spite of what he sees or feels. The new believer must believe the Word, must speak the Word (2 Corinthians 4:13), and must walk the Word, by faith and not by sight (2 Corinthians 5:7). He must understand what faith is and how it works. Our goal is to establish Bible thinking, believing, speaking and acting in the new believer, grounding him in the positive faith, confession and blessing of the truth of the Word of God.

Who am I in Christ?

1. Blessed: Ephesians 1:3; 2 Peter 1:3

2. A child of God: Romans 8:16; 1 John 3:2

3. A new creation: 2 Corinthians 5:17

4. Redeemed: Galatians 3:13

5. Righteous: Romans 5:19

6. Bold: Proverbs 28:1

What do I have in Christ?

1. Abundant life: John 10:9-10

2. Spiritual fruit: Galatians 5:22-23

3. Authority: Luke 10:19; John 1:12

4. Access: Romans 5:1-2; 1 John 2:1-2

5. Ability to overcome temptation: 1 Corinthians 10:13; 1 John 5:4-5; Hebrews 4:14-16

What can I do in Christ?

1. Walk in victory: Romans 8:1-4

2. Understand the Word: John 16:13; I John 2:27

3. Pray with confidence: 1 John 5:14-15; Matthew 6:9-13

Pray specific, so when you get blessed you'll know it was him

4. Be faithful: Galatians 5:22-23

Once you decide to do something do it.

5. Witness with power: Romans 1:16

Share others.

6. Fellowship: 1 John 1:3

Notes

Study Questions: Essential Two

1. What is the Second Essential for spiritual maturity? The Word of God

2. What is the confession that a believer can make after being grounded in this Second Essential?

3. From the introduction of the first outline, we see that the Bible is the Word of God and as the Word of God it is also five things. What are they? As the Word of God, the Bible is:
Alive, food, authority, food

4. From "How and where to begin," what are the three things you must have to understand and benefit from the wisdom of the Bible?

5. What is the key ingredient to benefiting from the Word?

    Obedience

6. What does it mean to "make a good confession?"

    To say the same thing that the Lord says "the word"

7. The three areas of a good confession are (Fill in the blanks): Who_____ in Christ? What _____ in Christ? What can _____ in Christ?

8. List as much of the good confession from the three areas that you recall.

    _____

    _____

    _____

Essential Three
Prayer

Effective communion with the Lord is the emphasis of Essential Three. Three areas influence this communion - Abiding, Worship and Prayer. There is an outline on Abiding, a second on Worship and Prayer, and a third on the various kinds of prayer and the scriptural rules that govern their operation. The Kingdom Result of effective communion is God's dominion or rule in the hearts of men. Experientially, it is the will of God for the believer to walk under the authority of the Word of God in the anointing of the Holy Spirit. Our intent is to instruct the new believer in the practical how – to's of establishing God's dominion in his life. By simple definition, prayer is communing with God. There can be no lasting victory without this kind of spiritual interaction. Prayer begins with praise, continues with our talking to God about our needs and culminates in our hearing from God and establishing His kingdom. Prayer at its best is dialogue - we speak, God speaks.

The first outline (Outline 7) asks the question, "What does it mean to abide in Christ?" It takes a glimpse at the biblical prerequisites for abiding in Christ, the benefits of abiding in Christ, and the goal or purpose of abiding in Christ.

The second outline (Outline 8) has three parts. The first part answers the fundamental question, "Why do we worship?" One of the truths about worship seldom realized is that worship is a discipline. Though there are significant reasons and a benefit for worshipping, in the long run, the believer's success is because of his disciplined decision. As a spiritual priest (I Peter 2:5, 9), he must establish the praise habit and determine, as an act of his will, to minister unto the Lord.

The second part of Outline 8 answers the question, "How do we enter into God's presence?" The answer includes the listing of different kinds of praise with the scriptural references for them.

The third part of Outline 8 answers the fundamental question, "How do I pray effectively? What prayer format must I follow?" This section deals with the importance of prayer in the everyday life. There is a twofold goal of prayer: heavenward and earthward. The heavenward goals are ministering unto the Lord (worship) and conforming to the image of Christ (Romans 8:29; 2 Corinthians 3:18). The earthward goal is victory over the enemy and ministering to the lost. Make no mistake. This will only be accomplished when the people of God are effectively praying in order to see the goal of the kingdom of God established in the hearts of men.

The third outline (Outline 9) will look at the various kinds of prayer with the view of outlining the rules that govern their effective practice.

Most of us rely on our organizational skills or education in performing tasks, but the reality of kingdom building is that we can plant and water, but only God can make it grow (1 Corinthians 3:6). We can organize, we can intellectualize, but as the Scriptures say, "It is not by might, it is not by power, but it is by My Spirit, says the Lord" (Zechariah 4:6). This is not to say that organization and education are not necessary, for certainly, God is both organized and intelligent and we are to imitate Him (Ephesians 5:1).

However, we must also recognize that there is a spiritual power, which only comes through abiding in God's presence, biblical praise and worship, and believing prayer. It is that power which builds the Kingdom of God. It is that power which will make a difference in our lives. Practicing the presence of God in prayer, for the maturing believer, must be a priority. We must pray if we are to prevail.

The confession: I am in His presence praying
- communing.

Areas covered in this section:

7. Abiding: Definition, Benefits, Goals

8. Worship and Prayer: The Why of Worship, The How of Entering God's Presence, The How of Effective Prayer: The Lord's Prayer
9. Prayer: The Various Kinds

Outline 7. Abiding

"What does it mean to abide in Christ?" The word, "abide," means "to stay, to remain, and to live in." To abide in Christ, means that the believer has taken up residence in the Lord. He "lives in the Lord" - his faith in Christ is the source of his life. He is now a part of the Body of Christ. By faith, he has united himself with Christ in covenant relationship. Marriage is used to illustrate this union, this oneness and this permanence (Ephesians 5:31-32). Christ is his life (Colossians 3:3-4). This is a permanent covenant arrangement that is made possible by the shed blood of Jesus and our faith in Him. Jesus has called all believers to this reality of abiding.

> *I am the vine, you are the branches. If a man remains (abides) in Me and I in him, he will bear much fruit; apart from Me you can do nothing (John 15:5).*

As a new believer understands what it means to abide in Christ, the foundation for prayer is established. He is getting ready for the confession: "I am in His presence - communing."

A. What are the biblical prerequisites for abiding in Christ?

1. A simple salvation commitment to Jesus Christ, according to the Bible, which includes repentance from the practice of sin and wrongdoing, and the confession of faith in the lordship of Jesus Christ (Acts 20:21).

2. A salvation commitment that includes being baptized in water, obeying the Word and fellowshipping with believers (local church membership)

B. What are the benefits of abiding in Christ? (Psalm 91)

1. Salvation assurance (Romans 8:16-17); experiencing peace with God (Romans 5:1) and having the peace of God within (Philippians 4:7)

2. Spiritual power through the Holy Spirit (Acts 1:8)

3. Access to God in prayer (Psalm 34:15; John 15:7)

4. Divine protection (Psalm 34:7; 91:1-16)

C. What is the goal or purpose of abiding in Christ?

1. To reflect the likeness (Romans 8:29) and the glory (Romans 8:18; 2 Corinthians 3:18) of God's Son that He may be the firstborn among many brothers (Romans 8:29)

2. To establish the kingdom of God in the earth (Matthew 6:10) by being the salt of the earth and the lights of the world (Matthew 5:13-14); and by taking the gospel of the kingdom (dominion) into the entire world (Matthew 28:19: 24:14) and bearing fruit (John 15:1-8)

Notes

→ You want to be the <u>salt</u> of <u>the</u> <u>earth</u>.
Can people come to you?....
What is your flavor?
Do you bring light to others

Outline 8. Worship and Prayer

After understanding the truth of abiding, the new believer needs to know the why and the how of worship and prayer. True worship and effective prayer are powerfully connected and the new believer must operate effectively in both of these areas. Having the foundation stone of Prayer in his life prepares him for spiritual maturity. Being grounded in this level enables the new believer to boldly confess, "I am in His presence -communing."

A. Why do we worship?

1. Because God has commanded us to worship (Psalm 29:1-2; 33:1-2; 100:1-2). The Father seeks worship from His people (John 4:23-24).

2. Because, as the children of God who have the Holy Spirit (Romans 8:16; Galatians 4:6), it is natural for us to "minister unto the Lord" (Acts 13:2 KJV) as spiritual priests (I Peter 2:5, 9) and be filled with the Spirit through singing (Ephesians 5:18-19).

3. Because, as the redeemed of the Lord (Psalm 107:1-2), it is normal for us to praise God because of who He is and to thank God because of what He has done for us through Jesus Christ (Psalm 103:1-

6). This is the only sane response to God's loving-kindness. We are new creations (2 Corinthians 5:17) who have been given the gift of righteousness: right standing with God (Romans 5:17) and are able, through Jesus Christ (Hebrews 10:19-20), to stand in the presence of God.

4. Because we understand the power of praise - that God Almighty is enthroned in the midst of our praise (Psalm 22:3).

B. How do we enter into God's presence?

1. We enter God's presence through worship in Spirit and in Truth (John 4:23-24). Because God is Spirit, we worship Him "in spirit" - out of our spirit man, speaking and singing words of adoration to God with the assistance of the Holy Spirit who is within us, and "in truth" - according to the teachings of the Word of God. It is essential to be filled and stay with the Holy Spirit (John 4:23-24; Philippians 3:3; Ephesians 5:18-19).

2. We must know the different expressions of worship to God.

   a. Singing: Psalm 9:2, 11; 59:16; 81:1

b. Audible praise: Psalm 34:1; 103:1; I Corinthians 14:15; Revelation 19:1

c. Shouting: Psalm 47:1, 63:1-3; Joshua 6:5, 10, 16

d. Clapping: Psalm 47:1

e. Dancing: Psalm 149:3

f. Lifting hands: Psalm 63:4; 134:2; I Timothy 2:8

g. Bowing; prostrating, kneeling: Psalm 95:6; Ezra 9:5; Daniel 6:10

h. Musical instruments: Psalm 150:3-5; Revelation 14:2

Note-the bodily instruments of worship are:

- Mouth, voice (singing, shouting, praising)

- Hands, arms (clapping hands, lifting arms)

- Feet (dancing, leaping)

3. We come into the presence of God with psalms of praise and thanksgiving, hymns,

and spiritual songs. As the spirit of God moves upon us, our worship becomes a spontaneous expression of exalted (high) praise to God (Psalm 100:4; Colossians 3:16; Hebrews 2:12). Hallelujah! This is being filled with the Holy Spirit (Ephesians 5:18-19).

C. How do I pray effectively? What prayer format must I follow?

1. Establish a time and a place. The new believer will get nowhere by leaving something as important as worship and prayer to chance. If he cannot find time, he must make time to seek God. Next, he must choose a place of prayer in his house. Set it apart for that specific purpose. Having a place to go for prayer will increase his faithfulness and effectiveness.

2. The new believer must also have a plan. His devotional plan should include the study of the Word. (See Essential Two: Word; Outline 5; Section c). His plan for prayer must follow the prayer outline that the Lord has given us in Matthew 6:9-13, commonly known as "The Lord's Prayer." Jesus taught His disciples to pray using this prayer outline:

a. ***Our Father in heaven, hallowed be Your name.*** First, notice that throughout this prayer, the pronouns are all plural - "our and us." It goes beyond, "my" and "me" to "our" and "us." This means that this is a kingdom prayer. When the new believer prays this prayer, he or she should have in view the establishing of the Kingdom of God and should also recognize that prayer at its best is inclusive. This is being Kingdom Conscious. "hallowed be Your name" means - begin with bold, audible praise. Praise the Lord because of **who He is** (Psalm 48:1; Revelation 4:8). Worship God around His name (Psalm 8:1; 34:3; 103:1). Jesus taught His disciples to enter the presence of God calling Him "Father" and hallowing (exalting) His name. Included in this discipline is the new believer's understanding of who he is, what he has, and what he can do as one who is in Christ (Use the truth learned from Outline 6 under Essential Two). He should know that he is able to call God his "Father" because of the relationship he has with Him through faith in Christ. Jesus Christ is our great High Priest who has created access for us into the presence of God (Hebrews 4:14; 10:19-20).

b. **Your** *kingdom come, Your will be done on earth as it is in heaven.* Jesus teaches the new believer to establish the Kingdom of God as priority in his praying. He should begin by prayerfully examining himself in terms of the will of God being done in his daily life. Is he obedient to the Word? Is he seeking first the Kingdom of God? These are the kinds of questions that should be asked in this examination process. He begins, therefore, by praying for himself, examining himself, his walk and prioritizing the Kingdom in him first.

Next, he should pray (intercede) for the needs of others beginning with those who are closest to him and continuing to an ever-widening circle of his spheres of influence. For example, wife, children, parents, siblings, pastor of church, leaders of ministry, friends, saints in need, government officials (city, state, country, and world), etc. His focus should be that the Kingdom of God and the will of God will be established in the earth in people (1 Samuel 12:23; Ephesians 3:14-19; 1 Timothy 2:1-6). The specific areas, where God's Kingdom is to be established, are listed in the rest of the prayer (Matthew 6:11-13).

c. *Give us today our daily bread.* This means that the new believer should be specific in his prayer requests. "Daily bread" means basic needs. Paul says to make our needs known to God with thanksgiving (Philippians 4:6-7). The "thanksgiving" part is the faith side of prayer for basic needs. Since God has promised to meet our needs (Matthew 6:25-34), our praying with thanksgiving is praying in faith and believing God's promises. There is a peace, which comes when we specially pray with thanksgiving for our own needs (Philippians 4:7) and there is a power, which comes when we specifically pray (intercede) for the needs in the lives of others that we know. Praying in faith for our basic needs (daily bread) is simple because none of our basic needs (food, clothing, shelter, money, etc.) have a mind of their own. None of them can disagree with us, determining to withstand our faith in God's word, and not come to us.

Also, the new believer needs to be specific in his prayer requests. This may also require boldness, but specific requests brought to God indicate that the believer has faith. To pray generally about needs is not really praying in faith. A general request may be answered, but is difficult to prove. The result is that the believer's faith is not strengthened. But when he steps out in faith with a specific request and receives the answer, he knows that it is from God. Maturity comes with accepting that kind of prayer request responsibility.

d. ***Forgive us our debts, as we also have forgiven our debtors.*** This part of the prayer means that the new believer establishes the Kingdom of God in his interpersonal relationships. It requires examining himself in the area of forgiveness.

Jesus taught that the Father will not forgive us if we do not forgive others (Matthew 6:15). Walking in forgiveness is one of the basic requirements for walking in peaceful fellowship with others. Paul exhorts us,

If it is possible, as far as it depends on you, live at peace with everyone (Romans 12:18).

This requires practicing forgiveness as a lifestyle. For the new believer to pray in faith for peaceful, reconciled relationships is more difficult than simply praying for his basic needs. Remember basic needs (daily bread) do not have a mind of their own. But other people do. Their lack of faith or negative actions or attitudes can nullify the effects of his faith. He should not give up, however. He simply needs to exercise more tenacity and persistence in order to obtain victory.

e. ***And lead us not into temptation, but deliver us from the evil one.*** During this part of the prayer, the new believer is praying that the dominion of the Kingdom of God will come into the way he is being led. Kingdom of God come, will of God be done in this all-important area of being led. As our Shepherd, the Lord promises to lead and guide us to where we can lie down in green pastures beside quiet waters and be restored in paths of righteousness for His name sake (Psalm 23: 1-3). Jesus teaches us to pray that we will be delivered from the evil one (Satan), who seeks to overthrow us by temptation (Matthew 6:13). Instead, we are to seek to be led by the Spirit of God

Satan seeks us to turn our backs on God Lord thank you for your hedge of protection

(Romans 8:14) into all areas of truth (John 16:13).

This requires a fundamental desire to be in the center of the will of God; a desire to be used of God. Praying this part of the prayer is more difficult than the other two areas.

Again, your basic needs (daily bread) are easily met since basic needs have no will of their own and you need-basic faith. Walking in reconciled forgiveness with men who have a will of their own is more difficult, and you need – strong faith. Living in the center of God's will, while desiring to be used of God, is more difficult because of the opposition of a totally evil adversary. You will need – great faith.

f. *For yours is the Kingdom and the power and the glory forever.* Prayer should end as it begins; with praise. Giving God the glory is the most appropriate. The Kingdom is His and the power is His. All belongs to Him. Praying this at the end is simply recognition of the obvious. It is proper because it keeps everything in the proper perspective – away from self and centered in God.

Notes

Outline 9: What are the various kinds of prayer?

Most new believers assume that there is only one kind of prayer, and if they recognize that there are different kinds of prayer, they assume that they are all governed by the same rules. The truth is that there are various kinds of prayer with different rules or requisites governing each. This does not mean that there are no similarities. Of course some of the rules are the same, but some are different enough for the new believer to realize that to use the rules of one type of prayer with another could hinder their prayer's effectiveness. In the outline that follows, we will briefly summarize each kind of prayer and their governing rules or necessary requisites.

A. **The Prayer of Commitment.** Often called the sinner's prayer, the basic requisites for making this prayer commitment to God are:

1. The basic belief that God exists and will reward the diligent seeker (Hebrews 11:6).

2. Godly sorrow for sin that leads to genuine repentance (2 Corinthians 7:10) and faith in Christ Jesus (Acts 20:21).

3. The belief that Jesus is the Christ, the Son of the living God (Matthew 16:16) who died for our sins, according to the

Scriptures, and was raised from the dead (1 Corinthians 15:3-4), and the will to make Jesus Christ the Lord of your life (Romans 10:9).

B. The Prayer of Deliverance. Deliverance is the main focus of the ministry of Jesus (Matthew 1:21; Luke 4:18; John 8:31-36). During His earthly ministry, Jesus commissioned His disciples to minister deliverance to those who were bound (Matthew 10:8). He stated further that "driving out demons" is one of the signs that follow those who believe (Mark 16:17). Some requisite needs for those praying this prayer – The believer...

1. Needs to have made Jesus Christ Lord of his life and be filled with the Holy Spirit (Acts 19:13; Luke 24:49).

2. Needs to know that Jesus has all authority in heaven and on earth (Matthew 28:18).

3. Needs to know that Jesus disarmed all demons by His death on the cross (Colossians 2:15).

4. Needs to know that the name of Jesus has authority and power over all demons (Philippians 2:9-10).

5. Needs to know that he has been given authority over demon spirits in the name of Jesus (Luke 10:17:19).

6. Needs to know that he must boldly command demon(s) to leave in the name of Jesus (Acts 16:18).

7. Needs to know the importance of ministering deliverance with the help of others; Jesus sent them out by two (Luke 10:1). One should address the demon while the other(s) pray (Mark 9:29). And finally, it is important to get the person to whom he is ministering to agree with him (Matthew 18:19). When possible, he should take the time to teach the person needing deliverance, what the Bible says about deliverance in the name of Jesus.

C. **The Prayer of Binding and Loosing.** The teaching of Jesus on this type of prayer is found in Matthew and in Mark. In Matthew 12:29 and the parallel passage in Mark 3:27, Jesus is teaching about binding the enemy – demon spirits. In this regard, the new believer would "bind" the demon (Matthew 12:29; Mark 3:27), meaning – he would command the demon to stop his evil activity and be quiet, and "loose" the believer for whom he is praying (Matthew 18:18; see also

16:19), meaning – free them to experience the blessing of freedom and deliverance.

Finally, while the truth of Matthew 18:18 is applicable to deliverance, contextually, the passage has to do with solving a kind of local church conflict. The "binding and the loosing" refer to men not demons. Clearly, the local church, as it stands in agreement (vs. 19), has the authority to bind or loose an unruly member. An example of this is found in 1 Corinthians 5:4-7. Some rules for this are:

1. A local church member can be expelled by the Pastor, the elders, or the leaders of the congregation because of a witnessed, sinful action or attitude (Matthew 18:17). This is church discipline, where the entire church agrees not to have fellowship with a wayward member (1 Corinthians 5:11; Romans 16:17).

2. The purpose for this discipline is twofold: (1) to rid the local church of defilement (1 Corinthians 5:6-7, 13), and (2) to bring the offender to repentance (1 Corinthians 5:5; 2 Corinthians 2:6-11; 7:8-10). Remember, the goal of church discipline is restoration (Galatians 6:1).

D. **The Prayer of Faith.** Obviously, there is no prayer without faith (Hebrews 11:6). All legitimate prayer is made in faith. This specific "prayer of faith" has reference to James 5:15 which is a prayer for physical healing. The rules or requisites for this are:

1. Faith must be exercised by the person who is sick. He or she must call for the elders of the church to come and pray (James 5:14).

2. Faith requires that the one praying believes that God has promised to heal believers (James 5:15; Isaiah 53: 4-5; 1 Peter 2:24). He must believe that healing is the will of God for His people (Exodus 15:26; 23:25).

3. Praying the prayer of faith for healing requires that the one praying believes before he sees a physical manifestation (2 Corinthians 1:20; 5:7).

4. Those praying can anoint the sick one with oil in the name of the Lord (James 5:15; Isaiah 53:4-5; 1 Peter 2:24). He must believe that healing is the will of God for His people (Exodus 15:26; 23:25).

5. The prayer of faith can mean that the believer ministers the word of God's healing provision simply through the laying on of hands and speaking the Word.

Jesus ministered this way (Mark 1:41-42;
3:5; 7:33-34; Luke 7:14-15; John 5:6-9).

6. The prayer of faith can be used to pray
for other things (Hebrew 11:1) besides
healing, but the believer must be careful
that those things are promised in the
Word of God. Faith is active when the
Word is present (Romans 10:17).

E. **The Prayer of Agreement.** This prayer
requires the full agreement of at least two
believers. It is based upon the teaching of
Jesus in Matthew 18:19. From the passage
the requirements are:

1. At least two "living" believers (one
cannot be in heaven) must agree in prayer
for the same thing.

2. The "anything you ask for" must be
understood in the light of other passages
such as 1 John 5:14-15. To agree in
prayer, in faith, means that the believers
are praying according to the will of God
and the Word of God, expecting that God
will intervene.

F. **The Prayer of Dominion.** This is the prayer
that Jesus taught His disciples to pray, which
is commonly called "The Lord's Prayer"
(Matthew 6:9-13). "The Lord's Prayer" is a

prayer outline that Jesus taught his disciples to use. It is a prayer of dominion, a prayer where the dominion or rule of the Kingdom of God is established. The prayer has two main sections: (1) Worship – establishing His name (Matthew 6:9); and (2) Dominion – establishing His Kingdom (Matthew 6:10-13). The requisites or needs for this prayer are:

1. The one praying must be born again (John 3:3, 5), have a relationship with God the Father (Matthew 6:9), know Jesus Christ as his Lord (Romans 10:9), and walk in holiness (Psalm 24:3).

2. The believer must know the power of true worship (John 4:23-24; Psalm 22:3; 100:1-4).

3. The believer must understand that the purpose of being in God's presence is to be empowered to establish the glory of His Kingdom in the earth and in every sphere of his influence (Matthew 6:10-13). Filled with the power of His presence, he boldly pronounces, "Come Kingdom of God! Be done will of God!"

G. **The Prayer for Guidance.** The psalmist called the LORD our Shepherd (Psalm 23:1) and apostle Paul taught that to be led by the

Spirit of God is to be a child of God (Romans 8:14). Mature believers seek the Lord's guidance through prayer. The requisites or needs for this prayer are:

1. The believer must have the assurance that he is a child of God (John 1:12; Romans 8:16-17).

2. The believer must be filled with the Holy Spirit (Acts 1:8).

3. The believer must be totally surrendered to the will of God, being willing to say, "Not my will, but as the Lord wills."

Many mistakenly try to use this rule of the Prayer for Guidance, praying, "If it be Thy will," in areas where the will of God is clearly spelled out in the Word. The Prayer of Faith, for example, is rendered powerless by the phrase, "If it be Thy will," because faith believes that the promise, as an expression of the will of God, is sure (Romans 4:16). While the phrase, "If it be Thy will," is most appropriate for use in seeking God's guidance, it is out of place and indicates a lack of faith when used in areas where the will of God is clearly expressed in scriptures. For example, no one in his right biblical mind would counsel someone wanting to be saved to pray The Prayer of Commitment saying, "Lord, come into my life and save me ... if it be Thy will," because of the truth of 2 Peter 3:9.

4. The believer must desire to be lead and used by God (Philippians 2:13).

Notes

Study Questions: Essential Three

1 What is the Third Essential for Spiritual Maturity?

_____

_____

2 What is the confession that a believer can make after being grounded in the Third Essential?

_____

_____

3 What are two of the four benefits of abiding in Christ?

_____

_____

_____

4 Establishing the foundational stone of Prayer in your life means creating the realization that you are always in the _____ _____ of God.

5 What is the only fitting response to this truth of His loving - kindness?

_____

_____

_____

6 You can know the reality of daily worship by (2 things):

_____

_____
_____

7 The perfect outline for prayer that the Lord Jesus Christ taught His disciples is commonly called

_____
_____

Where is it found in the New Testament (book, chapter and verses)?

_____
_____

8 To experience peaceful fellowship with others, we must learn how to

_____
_____

9 List some of the various kinds of prayer:

_____
_____
_____

Essential Four
Fellowship

The essence of "Christian Fellowship" within the covenant community of the local church is developing a godly, caring, loving relationship between brothers and sisters in Christ. This relationship creates the sense of being responsible for one another, or being your brother's keeper. The by-product of this kind of caring and sharing is spiritual maturity.

The first outline of Essential Four (outline 10) asks, "What is a covenant community?" The primary purpose of the covenant community is to be the reflection, on earth, of the will of God in heaven. This means that the world should see the purposes of God being fulfilled within the Church. The promises that the Father has made, the price that the Son paid, the power that the Holy Spirit has imparted, and the plan of discipleship that the Lord has set in motion, all speak of the purposes of God's glory combined to accomplish the will of God on earth – the uniting of all things in Christ (Ephesians 1:9-10). The basic truth that believers need each other in order to do the work of God on earth is the underlying theme of this outline. The new believer is not complete and cannot be fully mature without the fellowship of other Christians.

The second outline (outline 11) asks, "What do the ordinances mean?" The ordinances dealt with are – Water Baptism and The Lord's Supper and I have also included a section on Feet Washing. While many churches don't recognize this as a formal ordinance, I believe that this discipline is essential to spiritual maturity for several reasons and I will share these reasons in the outline. The outline of each ordinance will help the new believer understand the biblical meaning of the ordinances and why we practice them. The believer should take the time to look up all of the Scriptures in each area. Because it is only an outline, it is not as thorough in its explanation as prose, but the experienced teacher will easily understand the references and their meanings as applied to the different sections.

The third outline (outline 12) asks, "How do I grow the Fellowship of the local church?" The answer in one sentence is – by total commitment, agreement, submission, and support. The key word is *total*. God does not use part - time believers. While an argument may be for the salvation of those who are partially committed, submitted, etc., it is clear that God really uses only those who are totally sold out for Him. Knowing this truth will strengthen the new believer's ability to discern who the mature are.

Total surrender will give him a rod for measuring maturity within the body, and determining whom he will emulate. Ministry within the local church is so important. Most do not realize what is at stake when they take for granted or make light of important things like fellowship, agreement, submission, and support. My desire is to place a strong emphasis on the superior goal of the anointing of unity. The key to that understanding is the truth of Psalm 133.

The Confession: I am in Covenant – Sharing.

Areas Covered in this Section:

10. What is a covenant community? The New Covenant, the Church of God - universal and local.
11. What do the Ordinances mean: Baptism, the Lord's Supper, and Feet Washing?
12. How do I grow in the Fellowship of the local church?

Outline 10. What is a covenant community?

Setting the foundation stone of Fellowship in the life of the new believer will necessitate an understanding of the importance of covenant. When we experience the new birth, we are born again into the family of God. This family consists of brothers and sisters who are in covenant with each other. They have come out of the world (2 Corinthians 6:17-

18), unto the Lord Jesus (Matthew 11:28), and into the Kingdom (Colossians 1:13). Because they all have the same Lord, are washed in the same blood, are obedient to the same Word, are filled with the same Spirit, and pray to the same heavenly father, they are brethren, and they have what the Bible calls *fellowship*.

A. **The definition** – A covenant community is a fellowship of born again believers who have established - covenant together. They are committed to the Lordship of Jesus Christ, obedient to His Word, and determined to share their life and resources with each other. They love each other. They understand the Lord's command to seek first the Kingdom.

1. **Their commitment to the Lord is *total*** (Luke 9:23; 14:26-33). This is more than someone just "committing his life to the Lord." It is where he surrenders so totally to the Lordship of Jesus Christ that Jesus actually begins to live His *life* out through him (see Galatians 2:20).

2. **Their obedience to the Word is *uncompromising*** (Acts 2:42). They have foundational stability and strength as a result of being doers of the Word and being guided by the Holy Spirit (Matthew 7:24-25; Romans 8:14).

3. **The determination to share is *unselfish*** (Acts 2:44-45). They have made a covenant commitment to share their life and resources with the brethren within the Fellowship. This commitment is based upon love. The Kingdom of God is established in this covenant – sharing atmosphere. The Greek word, "fellowship," in the New Testament literally means, "sharing in common." Sharing in common in the average local church is not common, but it should be. The New Testament church does not exist without this level of intimate interaction. In practice, this is what fellowship is.

4. **Their desire to serve is *genuine*** (1 John 2:6; Matthew 20:28). It is based upon humility (Matthew 20:26-27), which has as its perspective, reconciliation and discipleship (2 Corinthians 5:18-20; 2 Timothy 2:2).

B. **The Church** – God's new covenant community promise to the world is **universal.** It includes all of the redeemed, and it is seen and experienced in **local** assemblies.

1. **The promise.** *"The Time is coming when I will make a New Covenant!" (Jeremiah 31:31-34; Hebrews 8:7-13)* The promise of the New Covenant was made hundreds

of years before Jesus came to establish it at His first advent.

2. **The proclamation.** *"Upon this rock I will build My church!" (Matthew 16:18-20)* This proclamation by Jesus is evidence of the new order of the new covenant.

3. **The price.** *"Be shepherds of the church of God, which He bought with His own blood!" (Acts 20:28b)* The price for the New Covenant was the precious blood of the Lord Jesus Christ.

4. **The power.** *"You will receive power when the Holy Spirit comes on you; and you will be My witnesses in Jerusalem, and in all Judea and Samaria, and to the ends of the earth! (Acts 1:8)* The power to effectuate the New Covenant comes from the anointing of the Holy Spirit.

5. **The plan.** *"Therefore go and make disciples of all nations, baptizing them in the name of the Father and of the Son and of the Holy Spirit, and teaching them to obey everything I have commanded you. And surely I am with you always, to the very end of the age!" (Matthew 28:19-20)* The plan that Jesus instituted for the salvation of the world, the establishing of

the New Covenant, is simply – the discipling of men.

6. **The purpose.** *"And glory of the LORD will be revealed, and all mankind together will see it. For the mouth of the LORD has spoken!" (Isaiah 40:5)* The glorious purpose of the New Covenant community is to be the reflection of His glory in the earth. The Kingdom of God in the earth mirrors the will of God in heaven and we are literally transformed by that level of interaction. Paul said,

And we, who with unveiled faces all reflect the Lord's glory, are being transformed into His likeness with ever increasing glory, which comes from the Lord, who is the Spirit. (2 Corinthians 3:18)

Notes

Outline 11. What do the Ordinances Mean?

The term "ordinance" is used to denote a sacred observance that the Lord ordered us to practice. Jesus ordered us to teach the disciples we make to "obey everything I have commanded you. And surely I am with you always, to the very end of the age" (Matthew 28:20). This is an outline of those "ordered" things and what they mean. There are two such sacred ordinances: Water Baptism and The Lord's Supper (Communion), but I have included a third, Feet Washing.

A. Water Baptism (Greek: βαπτίζω (baptizdo) literally means "to dip, to immerse")

1. **Why do we baptize today?**

a. Because Jesus, the head of the Church, was baptized (Matthew 3:13-17) and the church is his body (Ephesians 1:22-23). If the head was baptized, the body, of necessity, must also be baptized.

b. Because Jesus commanded us to baptize believers as a part of the process of making disciples (Matthew 28:19-20).

> c. Because the New Testament church practices baptism (Acts 2:38, 41; 8:12, 36-38; 10:47-48; 19:5).

2. What does the immersing of a believer mean?

The new believer must understand that God often "pictured" spiritual truth by using natural events in history. Time and again, in the Old Testament, God would fashion the events in the lives of the children of Israel to teach them and *us* spiritual truth. For example, the smiting of the rock (Exodus 17:6) equals the crucifixion of Christ and the water flowing out of the rock represents salvation coming through Christ to us (John 4:13-14). Paul said that the rock was Christ (1 Corinthians 10:4). The lifting up of the snake in the desert and the physical healing for Israel from poisonous snake bites (Number 21:8-9) equals the lifting up of Christ on the cross and the spiritual healing that results in exercising faith to *look and live* (John 3:14). Thus, in the Old Testament, God frequently illustrated spiritual reality by historical example.

In like manner, today God has painted a picture full of spiritual meaning in baptism. As before, God is illustrating spiritual reality by a physical event. The blessings of salvation are received by faith alone, and water baptism forms an integral part of that New Testament faith.

In fact, baptism confirms the genuineness of the faith exercised by the believer when he confesses Jesus as Lord. Through this physical act of obedience, he illustrates the spiritual blessings already received by faith.

    a. Baptism means burial. The new believer identifies with the crucifixion and burial of Christ. He is saying by being buried in a watery grave that his "old man" is dead, crucified with Christ (Romans 6:3-10; Galatians 2:20).

    b. Baptism means resurrection. The new believer identifies with the resurrection of Christ. He is saying by coming up out of the watery grave of baptism that he is a "new creation" and that he is "walking in newness of life" (2 Corinthians 5:17; Romans 6:3-10).

    c. Baptism means that the old is gone and the new is here. Baptism represents what the Scriptures call *spiritual circumcision,* the removing of a stony heart and putting on a heart of flesh, which is the new birth (John

3:3-5; Ezekiel 36:26; Romans 2:29; Colossians 2:11-12).

B. The Lord's Supper

1. **What is the Lord's Supper and what should it mean to me?** The term, the "Lord's Supper," taken from 1 Corinthians 11:20 refers to the covenant meal that believers eat together: it seals their unity, loyalty, and love for each other. Paul said that in partaking, believers *"proclaim the Lord's death until He comes"* (1 Corinthians 11:26). This means that the good news of the cross of Christ and the Kingdom of God can be seen by their covenant unity. The physical body of Jesus was broken on the cross so that that Body of Christ, universal and local, might be whole (united).

Also, the blood of Jesus was shed to create the New Covenant community where believers are forgiven and reconciled to God as new creations in Christ. Thus, the covenant community walks in forgiveness, reconciliation, loyalty, and love with each other. This is new covenant life in Christ and this covenant meal, The Lord's Supper, is a binding part of that new covenant life.

2. **Why should we be careful to take the Lord's Supper?** Jesus ordered the Church to partake of this meal "in remembrance of Him" (1 Corinthians 11:24-25). As believers reverently obey, remembering how and why Jesus lived and died, they are spiritually strengthened.

3. **What should be remembered about His life?** His love, the quality of His compassion for the poor and the oppressed, and the totality of His commitment to serve (Matthew 9:36; Luke 4:18-19), should be remembered. Remember that Jesus was born our Savior (Luke 2:11; Matthew 1:21). Remember that His coming fulfilled the prophecy of Immanuel – which means, "God with us" (Matthew 1: 22-23).

4. **What should be remembered about His death?** The sacrificial nature of His love, His broken body, and His shed blood should be remembered (John 10:11-18; 1 Corinthians 1:23-26). Also His resurrection and second coming should be remembered (1 Corinthians 15:3-4; 1 Thessalonians 4:16-17).

5. **What should be the reaction of believers at the Lord's Supper who have remembered His life and death?** They should examine themselves in the area of

covenant relationships (1 Corinthians 11:27-32). This means judge their broken relationships, realizing that the Lord's Supper is a "love feast" – a covenant meal, which is a seal of the New Covenant. You extend your hands in fellowship to the covenant family saying, "I love you. I am in covenant together with you. I will be loyal to you." This is what is meant by, "recognizing the body of the Lord" (1 Corinthians 11:29). Brokenness must be mended and breaches restored.

3rd Ordinance – **C. Feet Washing**

1. **Definition** – The spiritual practice ordered by the Lord where believers wash one another's feet (John 13:12-17). You are saying by doing it, *"I am among you as one who serves"* (Luke 22:27).

2. **There are four reasons why this should be practiced:**

   a. Jesus washed His disciples' feet (John 13:3-17).

   b. Jesus exhorted His disciples (we are included) to wash one another's feet (John 13:13-15).

c. The kingdom principle of greatness teaches that the "way up is down." We are commanded to humble ourselves (Matthew 20:26-27; Philippians 2:3-4; 1 Peter 5:5-6).

d. There is a blessing of joy attached to practicing this ordinance (John 13:17). And remember, *"The joy of the LORD is your strength"* (Nehemiah 8:10).

Notes

Outline 12. How do I grow in the Fellowship of the local church?

The Greek word, κοινωνία (koinonia), translated most often by the English word, "fellowship," in the New Testament, literally means, "sharing in common." Members of the local church have determined to "share together in common" the everyday things of life. When the new believer commits to this level of sharing, he lays this foundation stone of Fellowship in his life and makes a great step towards spiritual maturity. The following exhortations will assist the new believer in positioning himself for blessing; therefore, take a special note of them. The key word is **total**.

A. Total submission to the biblical authority of the pastor: *"Render to Caesar what is Caesar's"*

   1. What is the nature of pastoral authority? The pastor's delegated authority begins and ends with the Scriptures. Any spoken Word must agree with the prior revelation of the written Word of God.

      a. The pastor, as an example, qualifies himself by calling and by character (1 Timothy 3:1-7; Hebrews 5:4; 13:7).

      b. The pastor, as an overseer, watches over and warns his flock (Ezekiel

33:7; Hebrews 13:17) and protects them (Acts 20:28-31).

   c. The pastor, as a shepherd, nurtures and cares for his flock (1 Peter 5:2-4).

2. What should your attitude be toward that authority?

   a. Prayerful (Hebrews 13:18a)

   b. Submissive, Obedient (Hebrews 13:17)

B. Total agreement with the vision of the ministry:

1. Knowing that agreement brings God's power and God's anointing (Psalms 133; Matthew 18:19)

2. Knowing that agreement requires structure (Amos 3:3)

3. Knowing that agreement is strengthened through submission (Hebrews 13:17): The people must submit to the vision and direction of the leader. With the leader leading, the house is set in order. The majority must be taught to follow. The choir, for example, follows the direction of the leader. The same is true of the captain and his ship. (Wisdom

dictates: It is easier for ten men to submit to the vision of one man than for one man to submit to the visions of ten men.)

C. Total commitment to the fellowship of the saints:

   1. **Being an example within the flock** (Ephesians 5:8-21)

   2. **Sharing your life and resources** (Acts 2:44-45)

D. Total support of the work in the vineyard:

   1. **By your time** – the new believer is to use whatever gifts and talents he possesses to bless and support the Kingdom work.

   2. **By your talent and ministry** – the fruit of the new believer's witnessing in the world (among family, friends, and neighbors) will be channeled to the kingdom work (Acts 2:46-47).

   3. **By tithes, offerings and sacrificial giving** – the financial resources of the new believer's money, car and home (all possessions) are included in his total support of the work in the vineyard (Malachi 3:8-12).

Notes

Study Questions – Essential Four

1. What is the Fourth Essential for Spiritual Maturity?

   _____

   _____

2. What is the confession that a believer can make after being grounded in Essential Four?

   _____

   _____

   _____

3. Briefly define a covenant community.

   _____

   _____

   _____

4. Those in covenant with each other have a commitment to the Lord that is _____, obedience to the Word that is _____ _____, determinations to the Word that are _____, and a desire to serve humanity that is _____ _____.

5. Who paid the price for this covenant and what was the price? (Acts 20:28)

_____

_____

_____

6. What are the two ordinances? What is the third practice that I added? Why?

_____

_____

_____

_____

7.　　The Greek word, κοινωνία (koinonia), translated into the word "fellowship," literally means

_____

_____

8. To grow in the Fellowship of the local church requires total submission to the (Hebrews 13:17)

_____

9. Your total support for the work in the vineyard of the local church can be seen in what three areas?

_____

_____

_____

Essential Five
Followship

A covenant community is the bride of Christ (Ephesians 5:23) and has been established by the Word of God to accomplish God's will on earth as it is in heaven (Matthew 6:10). Nevertheless, too often churches try to use worldly orders and systems to accomplish their divine task. What is adopted and followed by many churches is a secular form of governance. God's word clearly says, "*obedience is better than sacrifice*" (1 Samuel 15:22). When Joshua succeeded Moses as the leader of the children of Israel, God told Joshua that the most important thing he needed to do was to obey His word. "*Be careful to obey all the law my servant Moses gave you; do not turn from it to the right or to the left, that you may be successful wherever you go*" (Joshua 1:6). God told Joshua that strict obedience to His word was the only way that he would be successful and experience His glory and favor like Moses did. Despite this biblical mandate, many churches follow the world and because of this, they struggle and fail to experience true biblical authority and divine power. The intent of Essential Five is to instruct believers in the true biblical governance that they and their local church should follow in order to experience God's supernatural power individually and corporately.

The first outline (Outline 13) asks the question, "What is biblical governance?" It explains the definition of biblical governance and how God operates in his biblical governance. The second outline (Outline 14) highlights the benefits of following God's biblical governance and the third outline (Outline 15) deals with the consequences of not following God's biblical governance. Unfortunately, so many of us are living with these consequences because we are either willfully or unknowingly violating God's biblical governance. The intent of this outline is to help the believer understand the negative consequences in order for them to choose to live under God's biblical governance and experience breakthrough and blessedness because of making the right decision.

The Confession: I am in submission – obeying.

The Areas Covered in the Section:

13. What is Biblical Governance?
14. What are the benefits of following God's biblical governance?
15. What are the consequences of not following God's biblical governance?

Outline 13. What is Biblical Governance?

Let all things be done decently and in order. (1 Corinthians 14:40)

God has an established order for his people. Our responsibility is to not only obey what His word tells us to do, but we must also obey how his word tells us to do it. Withstanding this, every believer must understand and obey Biblical Governance – God's established order.

A. **The Definition**. Democracy is the term used to describe the form of government we live by in the United States. A democracy is a form of government that recognizes that ultimate authority belongs to the people, who have the right to participate in the decision-making process and to appoint and dismiss their rulers. "Democracy" is derived from a Greek word meaning, "rule by the people." While a democracy is the established governance for the United States, it is not the established governance for God's order or his covenant community. God's biblical governance is a Theocracy. The word, Theocracy, originates from the Greek word theokratia. Theokratia is comprised of two Greek words: θεος (theos), which means "God," and κρατειν (kratein), which means "to rule." Therefore, while democracy means to "rule by the people," theocracy means to "rule by God." The order and governance that God established for us to follow in his Holy Word is a Theocracy.

1. **God's original design and desire for mankind was an unmediated Theocracy.** (Genesis 3)

   God created Adam and Eve and established theocratic order. They were simply supposed to follow the laws that God established about the Garden of Eden. The way that the serpent deceived Eve was by getting her to disobey God's theocracy and convincing her to follow her own order. (Genesis 3:1-4)

2. **God's design and desire for the Children of Israel was a Theocracy.** (Deuteronomy 4)

   The biggest stipulation and mandate from God that the children of Israel had to follow in order to reach the promise land and be successful, was to unwaveringly follow God's law. (Deuteronomy 4:1-2)

3. **God created "Judges" to direct the Children of Israel back to God's Theocracy.** (Judges)

   Every time the Israelites followed their own order they got into tremendous trouble. When they repented and returned to God's theocracy, God would deliver them from their problems. (Judges 3:7-9 & Judges 21:25)

4. **When we don't follow God's Theocracy, we reject God.** (1Samuel)
   When the Children of Israel desired a monarchy instead of a theocracy, they rejected God. (1Samuel 8:6-19)

5. **Jesus' death reestablished and solidified God's Theocracy.**
   When Jesus died on the cross, the veil in the temple was torn, symbolizing the direct access that we now have to God. (Matthew 27:50-51, Hebrews 4:14-16 & 7:26-27)

B. **How Does God Operate in His Biblical Governance?** Psalm 133 is the explanation of how God moves in a very distinct way within His governance. While this verse is often quoted and memorized by fraternal and civic organizations, this verse is a metaphor for how God operates within His governance.

How good and pleasant it is when brothers live together in unity! It is like the precious oil poured on the head, running down on the beard, running down on Aaron's beard, down upon the collar of his robes... (Psalm 133 NIV)

1. **It begins with the Pastor.** "*It is like the precious oil poured on the head, running down on the beard, running down on Aaron's beard...*" Aaron was the first priest (pastor) for the nation of Israel. (Exodus 29:1-9) God's governance always begins with the Priest/Pastor. Notice where the anointing oil is poured, it is poured upon the head.

2. **It moves to the People.** "*...running down on Aaron's beard, down upon the collar of his robes...*" The priest wore an Ephod and a breastpiece (Exodus 28:6-30). On the breastpiece were twelve stones that represented the Twelve Tribes of Israel. Therefore, when the anointing oil moved down from the head and beard of Aaron, it would cover the Ephod and breastpiece. In other words, God anoints the pastor and then the people. Yet notice that in order for the people to be anointed they have to be connected to the Pastor.

Notes

Outline 14 – What are the benefits of following Biblical Governance?

The word of God clearly reveals that there are tremendous benefits that come with following God's order. The intent of this outline is to highlight these benefits in order for the new believer to understand what's in store for them when they obey God's order.

A. Victory over difficulties (Exodus 17:8-16) - As long as the Israelites followed God's order, they were victorious.

B. Obtain the blessings God has for you (Joshua 1) - After Moses died, they were able to move into the promised land as long as they followed God's order.

C. Supernatural Power over evil spirits, disease and sickness (Matthew 10) - The disciples were given this power because they followed Christ.

D. Signs and Wonders (Acts 2:42-47) - The manifestation of signs and wonders occurred in the New Testament church because they submitted to God's order.

Notes

Outline 15 - What are the consequences of not following God's Biblical Governance?

We don't like to talk about it, but the reality is that there are real consequences for not following God's order. Too often believers don't experience the blessings of God and are not able to walk in their Divine Authority because they are out of order. The intent of this outline is to educate the believer about the consequences, in order for the believer to know better and do better.

- **A. Angering God and loosing His favor** (Exodus 32)

- **B. Sickness and disease** (Numbers 12:1-12)

- **C. No promotion and blessing** (Numbers 13:26 - Numbers 14)

- **D. Destruction and death** (Numbers 16)

- **E. No spiritual power** (Mark 9:14-35)

Notes

Study Question – Essential Five

1. What is the Fifth Essential for spiritual maturity?

_____

_____

2. What is the confession that a believer can make after being grounded in the Fifth Essential?

_____

_____

_____

3. What is the name of God's Biblical Governance?

_____

_____

_____

4. What is the difference between God's Biblical Governance and the United States Governance?

_____

_____

_____

5. God's Governance begins with the

_____?

6. What are some of the benefits of following God's Governance?

_____

_____

_____

7. What are some of the consequences of not following God's Governance?

_____

_____

_____

Essential Six
Stewardship

This essential is designed to disciple the believer not only in their faith, but also in their finances. Too often in today's culture, we develop lop-sided believers. These are believers that can pray, worship and work in ministry, but they do not honor God with their finances. Far too often we allow Jesus to be Lord in every area of our life except our finances. Believers must understand that they cannot over-emphasize certain areas of their faith and under-emphasize others. God is just as concerned about money as He is about other disciplines of our faith. This is evidenced by the fact that the Bible says more about money, than many other subjects. 16 of the 38 parables of Jesus Christ deal with how to handle money and possessions. In the bible there are 500 verses on prayer, fewer than 500 verses on faith, yet there are over 2,350 verses on money and possessions. The mature believer understands and follows what the bible says about money and possessions in addition to every other facet of life.

The first outline (Outline 16) deals with the question: What is Stewardship? In answering this question, the believer will understand why the bible teaches us that we don't really own anything and that one of the greatest, tangible signs of worship is how we handle what God has entrusted to us. The second outline (Outline 17) deals with the significance of Stewardship. It's not enough to know what Stewardship is without a clear understanding of its significance. Many believers have heard the word "Stewardship" or may be familiar with the concept, but they fail to practice it because they don't really understand how significant it is to our faith. This outline will teach you the profound significance of Stewardship so that you won't "perish because of a lack of knowledge" (Hosea 4:6). The final outline (Outline 18) will answer the question, "How do I practice stewardship?" The key ingredient is obedience, obedience, obedience!

The Confession: I am in His will – Giving.

Areas covered in this section:

16. What is stewardship?
17. The significance of stewardship.
18. How do I practice stewardship?

Outline 16. What is stewardship?

Everything that you have, you do not own! I know your name may be on the mortgage for your house or the title for your car, but you do not own it. Understanding this requires a radical paradigm shift because the world suggests; or would have you to think that what you posses, you alone own. While this is a popular worldview, it is not the truth supported by the Word of God. According to the Bible, we are not owners because:

A. God is the Owner: The bible clearly states that God is the sole owner of everything. *"Behold, to the Lord your God belong...the earth and all that is in it"* (Deuteronomy 10:14). *"The earth is the Lord's and all it contains"* (Psalm 24:1).

B. Specific Items that God owns:

1. **Land** (Leviticus 25:23) *"The land, moreover, shall not be sold permanently, for the Land is Mine."*

2. **Money** (Haggai 2:8) *"the silver is Mine, and the gold is Mine,' declares the Lord of Hosts."*

3. **Animals** (Psalm 50:10) *"For every beast of the forest is Mine, the cattle on a thousand hills."*

4. **All things** (1 Chronicles 29 11-14) *"Yours, O Lord, is the greatness and the power and the glory and the majesty and the splendor, for everything in heaven and earth is yours...Everything comes from you..."*

C. **Stewardship defined:** Stewardship is recognizing that God owns everything and that God has never transferred ownership of His creation to people (Colossians 1:17). Stewardship is the understanding that everything we have, God has entrusted or loaned to us. Therefore, we have the responsibility to handle what God has loaned to us in a way that pleases Him. The Greek word for steward is *"oikonomos,"* which can be translated into the English word "manager." In the bible, the position of steward is one of great responsibility and has full responsibility for all of his master's possessions.

Notes

Outline 17. What is the significance of stewardship?

When you understand and acknowledge that God owns everything, every financial decision becomes a spiritual decision. Understanding this means that the question is no longer, "Lord what do you want me to do with *my* money," but rather, "Lord what do you want me to do with *Your* money?"

A. Stewardship is significant because it requires that all of us as stewards do certain things:

   1. **Be faithful with what we are given.** The Lord requires us to be faithful regardless of how much He has entrusted to us. (Matthew 25:14-15)

   2. **Be faithful in every area.** God requires us to be faithful in how we handle 100 percent of His money. Not just 10 percent.

   3. **Be held accountable.** The Lord will hold us accountable for how we handle His money.

B. Stewardship has several advantages:

   1. **More intimate relationship with God.** We have the opportunity to enter into a

closer, more intimate fellowship with our Lord, as we are faithful with the possessions He has given to us. (Matthew 25:21)

2. **The development of character.** God uses money to refine our character. (Matthew 6:21)

3. **Having our financial house in order.** When we begin to operate according to God's plan for biblical stewardship, it will tremendously help our financial future. This will help us get out of debt, spend more wisely and save more effectively.

4. **Increase in material blessings.** Biblical stewardship will always result in material and financial increase for the steward. (Proverbs 11:24-25, 2 Corinthians 9:6-8)

Notes

Outline 18. How do I practice stewardship?

Understanding the concept of stewardship and its significance, the relevant question is how do we tangibly do this? Many believers will discuss stewardship, but many more need to actually practice it. This outline will teach you how. It begins with:

A. **The right attitude.** Practicing stewardship must first be done with the right attitude. This is what Paul was talking about in the book of *2 Corinthians:*

   I want each of you to take plenty of time to think it over, and make up your own mind what you will give. That will protect you against sob stories and arm-twisting. God loves it when the giver delights in the giving. God can pour on the blessings in astonishing ways so that you're ready for anything and everything, more than just ready to do what needs to be done. 2 Cor. 9:7-8 (MsgB)

   You cannot practice stewardship under compulsion. Practicing it under coercion renders it powerless. It is like saying thank you because someone is twisting your arm. When we act this way, it makes our giving insincere and ineffective. When you understand this principle and embrace it cheerfully, that's when the blessings of God rest upon your finances and your financial foundation is secured. The right attitude about steward-ship indicates two things:

1. **Our love for God.** 1 Corinthians 13:3 reads, "*If I give all my possessions to feed the poor...but do not have love, it profits me nothing.*" If we give off the wrong attitude, what we are saying to God is, "I don't love you." The Lord set the example of being motivated by love. "*For God so loved the world that He gave His only son*" (John 3:16). Notice the motivation, because God loved, He gave.

2. **Our worship of God.** Matthew 2:11 says, "On coming to the house, they saw the child (Jesus) with his mother, Mary, and they bowed down and worshipped him. Then they opened their treasures..." The height of the Magi's worship of Jesus involved giving. Far too often we think that giving is just something we do in a worship service. But that is not bibli-cally correct. The bible clearly explains that giving **IS** worship. This is why, while Jesus was in the temple during worship, he notices a woman in Mark chapter 12. He gathers the attention of his disciples and remarks that this woman just demon-strated extreme worship.

"Calling his disciples to him, Jesus said, "I tell you the truth, this poor widow has put more into the treasury than all the others. They all gave out of their wealth; but she out of her poverty put in everything – all she had to live on." Mark 12:43-44 (NIV)

B. The right actions. In 1 Corinthians 16:2 the Apostle Paul says, *"On the first day of every week let each one of you put aside and save, as he may prosper, that no collections be made when I come."* From this verse we glean instructions about how to give.

1. **Giving should be personal.** *"Let each of you…"* Every believer has the responsibility and privilege of giving.
2. **Giving should be periodic.** *"On the first day of every week"* The Lord requires us to give regularly. This is also why God instructs us to never appear before him empty-handed. (Exodus 23:15;34:20)
3. **Giving should be a private deposit.** *"Put aside and save…"* Giving to God should not be an afterthought, it should be your first thought. Before spending or paying bills, you ought to put aside the amount that you are giving to God.
4. **Giving should be premeditated.** Putting your giving amounts aside requires

planning. What you give should not be haphazard or last minute. (2 Corinthians 9:7)

C. The right amounts. There has been so much hype and hyperbole about what believers are biblically required to give. Some of the hyperbole has been in the attempt to not give what God requires. Some of the hype has been in an attempt to manipulate believers for the selfish gain of evangelists. This section of outline 18 will help you separate fact from fiction. Biblically, there are three categories of giving that God holds us accountable for:

1. **The Tithe.** The literal meaning of the word *tithe* is "a tenth" or ten percent. This word and concept is often misinterpreted today. Often people say they are "tithing" when they give five dollars a week, yet their annual income is $70,000. That is not a tithe! Five dollars a week is only a tithe when your weekly income is fifty dollars. The tithe is ten percent of your income. The tithe is **not optional**. The tithe is what we owe to God.

   A **tithe** of everything from the land, whether grain from the soil or fruit from the trees, **belongs** to the Lord; it is **holy** to the Lord. (Leviticus 27:30)

Because the tithe is not optional and the tithe is what we owe to God, failure to tithe brings negative consequences. This is why God is angry in the book of Malachi.

You people are robbing me, your God. And, here you are, asking, "How are we robbing you?" You are robbing me of the offerings and of the ten percent that belongs to me. That's why your whole nation is under a curse. I am the LORD All-Powerful, and I challenge you to put me to the test. Bring the entire ten percent into the storehouse, so there will be food in my house. Then I will open the windows of heaven and flood you with blessing after blessing. I will also stop locusts from destroying your crops and keeping your vineyards from producing. Everyone of every nation will talk about how I have blessed you and about your wonderful land. I, the LORD All-Powerful, have spoken! Malachi 3:8-12(CEV)

a. WHY SHOULD I TITHE? 8 REASONS FROM GOD'S WORD

i. Because God instructs us to.
"A tenth of all you produce is the Lord's, and it is holy." Lev. 27:30

ii. **Because Jesus instructed it as well.**
"Yes, you should tithe, and you shouldn't leave the more important things undone either." Matt. 23:23

iii.**Tithing demonstrates that God has 1ˢᵀ place in my life.**
"The purpose of tithing is to teach you to always put God in first place in your life." Deut. 14:23 (LB)

iv. **Tithing reminds me that everything I have was given to me by God!**
"Always remember that it is the Lord your God who gives you the ability to produce wealth." Deut. 8:18

v. **Tithing expresses my love for God.**
"How can I repay the Lord for all his goodness to me?" Ps. 116:12

"Each of you should bring a gift in proportion to the way the Lord your God has blessed you." Deut.. 16:17

vi.**God says that refusing to tithe is stealing from Him!**
"God says 'Will a man rob God? Yet you are robbing me!' But you ask, 'How do we rob you?' God says 'In tithes and offerings ... Bring your

whole tithe to My house.'" Mal. 3:8-10

vii. Tithing gives God a chance to prove He exists and wants to bless you!

*"Bring your whole tithe to My store-house. **Test me in this**" says the Lord, "and see if I will not throw open the floodgates of heaven and pour out **so much blessing** that you won't have room enough for it! I will prevent pests from devouring your crops and the vines in your fields will be protected from plagues."*   Mal. 3:10

viii. Tithing proves that I love God.

(Jesus) *"If you really love me, do what I command."*
John 14:15
"... I want you to be leaders also in the spirit of cheerful giving ... This is one way to prove that your love is real, that it goes beyond mere words."
2 Cor. 8:7b - 8 (LB)

b.   WHAT SHOULD I TITHE?

i. The first part of what I earn, not the leftovers.

*"Honor the Lord by giving him the **first part** of all your income."* Prov. 3:9-10

c. WHERE SHOULD I GIVE MY TITHE?

i. Where I physically worship.
*"Bring your **whole** tithe to My Storehouse (Temple) ..."*
Mal. 3:10

2. **The Offering.** The offering is a gift that goes above and beyond the tithe. The tithe is the beginning, basic and the bare minimum. The offering is the next level of giving after the tithe. Let me be clear, God does not honor your offering if you have not given your tithe. If I loan a friend $100.00 and he has not repaid the loan, that same friend cannot give me $50.00 and call it a gift. It is not a gift because he owes me. I cannot begin to receive a financial gift from him until he first repays me what he owes. This is the relationship between the tithe and the offering. (Deuteronomy 16:17; Luke 6:38)

3. **Sacrificial Giving.** This is the third category of giving that goes beyond normal giving. Biblically, this type of giving is called "sowing" or "first-fruit" giving. This type of giving involves much sacrifice and requires much faith, yet this type of giving yields tremendous rewards. (Deuteronomy 18:4; 2 Corinthians 9:6-7)

Notes

Study Questions – Essential Six

1. What is the Sixth Essential for Spiritual Maturity?

   _____

   _____

2. What is the confession that a believer can make after being grounded in Essential Six?

   _____

   _____

3. What is stewardship?

   _____

   _____

4. What are some of the advantages of stewardship?

   _____

   _____

   _____

5. Name a few of the biblical reasons we should tithe.

   _____

   _____

   _____

6. What are the three things that are required to practice stewardship?

_____

_____

_____

7. What are the three biblical categories of giving?

_____

_____

_____

Essential Seven
Ministry

The outlines in essential seven are designed to give the new believer some basic information about ministry. The goal is to create a maturity in him that will develop him into a ministry minded person. Remember the confession attached to this section is, "I am in ministry – serving." The backdrop of this section is ministry – servanthood.

The first outline (Outline 19) deals with the question: What are the three levels of the church's work? The answer is given in this outline with the three levels listed and defined. These levels are progressive: it begins with Evangelism, progresses into Follow-up and then into Discipleship. Jesus told the disciples that He would make them fishers of men (Mark 1:17). The progression of the three levels is seen as follows – after a believer catches a man (Evangelism), he teaches him the fundamentals in order to establish him in the Faith (Follow Up), and then, as the new convert proves himself to be faithful; you spend time building spiritual maturity and reproduction (Discipleship). These are the three levels of the church's work.

The second outline (Outline 20) asks the question: How do I prepare myself for working in the vineyard? The new believer should note that whenever we are dealing with the question of how, we are dealing with a valuable area. A worker is one who God uses to harvest souls in His vineyard. Jesus taught His disciples, *"The harvest is plenty but the workers are few"* (Matthew 9:37). This outline is designed to highlight the characteristics of a worker whom God uses. Five characteristics are given as keys to being used as workers in the vineyard. They are: desire, discipline, faithfulness, submission, and availability. All are powerful words, which should become pillars within the walls of the character of the new believer's Christian commitment. If the truths of this outline were to permeate the lives of all believers, the world would be won within our generation. The problem is not God's willingness to use us, but our willingness to measure up to His standards to be used. By God's grace, let us determine to go all the way.

The final outline (Outline 21) deals with the subject of servanthood. The confession of this section is, "I am in ministry, serving." Jesus demonstrated servanthood by His life (Matthew 20:28) and commissioned His disciples to operate in the same way (John 20:21). So the ultimate call of the believer is to be a servant. The blessing of servanthood is needed in the world and God has ordained that it comes through His church. This call to servanthood is explored again and again in this outline. My hope is that the truth of the final call will grip the hearts of every genuine believer who reads or hears this teaching.

The Confession: I am in Ministry – Serving.

The Areas Covered in this Section:

19. What are the three levels of the church's work? It is the fulfillment of the great Commission.
20. How do I prepare myself for laboring in the vineyard? To prepare God's people to be "fellow workers."
21. Servanthood: the ultimate call.

Outline 19. What are the three levels of the church's work?

There is a difference between the work of the church and church work. The former is ministry that is commissioned by God, while the latter is the traditional busy work in the church that is created by men. The local church will grow as the believers commit to being proficient in the following three areas of the work of the church:

A. Evangelism – The spiritual work of sharing the good news in the power of the Holy Spirit while trusting God to give the increase - The spiritual tools needed to succeed:

1. The Word (2 Timothy 2:15)

2. The Holy Spirit (Acts 1:8)

3. The love; compelling burden (Romans 5:5; 2 Corinthians 5:14)

B. Follow-up – The spiritual work of grounding the new believer in the Faith - The additional spiritual tools needed to succeed:

1. A clear and simple plan of focusing new believers toward making Christ their center

2. The example of dedicated, mature believers whose walk with the Lord is grounded and settled in the truth (Romans 12:1-2; Ephesians 4:14-16)

3. The will to nurture the new believer long enough to establish him in Christ (3-6 months on average)

C. Discipleship – The spiritual work of building spiritual maturity and spiritual reproduction in the life of a believer who is faithful - The additional spiritual tools needed to succeed:

1. The ability to discern who is faithful (Luke 6:12-16)

2. The understanding that mature disciples are called to transfer spiritual truth to faithful men (2 Timothy 2:2; Philippians 4:9)

3. The will to walk with a faithful believer long enough to reproduce yourself in him (2-5 years on average)

4. A clear understanding of the *7 Essentials For Spiritual Maturity* (Christ, Word, Prayer, Fellowship, Followship, Stewardship, and Ministry)

Notes

Outline 20. How do I prepare myself for laboring in the vineyard?

The characteristics for being used of God in His vineyard can be summarized in five words: Desire, Discipline, Faithfulness, Submission, and Availability. The new believer needs to have:

A. Desire

1. To imitate sainthood (Ephesians 5:1; 1 Corinthians 4:14-17; 11:1; Philippians 3:17; Hebrews 6:12)

2. To be used of God (Philippians 3:10-16)

B. Discipline

1. Of his time (Ephesians 5:15-16)

2. Of the appetites of the flesh (Romans 8:5-8; 1 John 2:15-16)

3. Of his thoughts (Proverbs 4:23; Philippians 4:8)

4. Of his words (Proverbs 18:21; Matthew 12:36-37; James 3:2)

5. Of his finances (Malachi 3:8-11; 1 Corinthians 16:2)

C. Faithfulness

1. In the daily worship of God, prayer, and surrender to the influence of the Holy Spirit (Ephesians 5:18-20; 6:18)

2. In the consistent study and memorization of the Word (Psalm 119:9-11; 2 Timothy 2:15; 1 Peter 3:15)

3. In the fellowshipping with God's people (Hebrews 10:25)

D. Submission

1. To the teaching, equipping, ministry of the pastor and other five-fold ministry gifts "to prepare God's people" (Ephesians 4:11-13)

2. To the collective ministry of the body as "fellow workers" (2 Corinthians 6:1)

E. Availability

1. To love (1 John 4:16b-18)

2. To help (1 Corinthians 12:28)

3. To serve (Matthew 20:28; Galatians 5:13)

4. To sacrifice (1 John 3:16)

5. To give (Luke 6:38; 2 Corinthians 9:6-9)

Notes

Outline 21. Servanthood - the ultimate call

Jesus set the pattern for servanthood by His own example. During His earthly ministry, He functioned as one who serves (Matthew 20:28) and He exhorted His disciples to do the same (Matthew 20:26-27). Just as Jesus was sent by the Father to serve, we are sent by the Son – to serve (John 20:21). Servanthood is our weapon, our crown, our goal and our life. There is no room for self-aggrandizement. It is servanthood, now and forever. The new believer is called to humble himself and serve, to become as a little child (Matthew 18:2-5) and serve. He is saved to serve, to throw off everything that hinders and sin that so easily entangles (Hebrews 12:1) and serve! Serve! SERVE!

A. I am in ministry – serving.

1. The new believer is born to serve the Lord (Colossians 3:24). As a spiritual priest, his first ministry is unto the Lord (1 Peter 2:5, 9).

2. The new believer is called to be patient, loving and united in the Spirit through the bond of peace with his brethren in his local church (Ephesians 4:1-3). In agreement, he serves with faithful brethren in the vineyard of Christ (2 Corinthians 6:1).

3. The new believer is commissioned to take the good news of the Kingdom into the entire world (Mark 16:15). To minister to the world means to serve the world.

B. **Washing feet** – The act of Jesus washing the feet of His disciples is an excellent example of the high calling to servanthood (John 13:1-17).

1. Feet washing means that the servant knows what power he has, where he has come from, and where he is going. (John 13:3)

2. Feet washing means that the servant is a part of the cleansing process of his brethren. (John 13:6-10)

3. Feet washing means that the servant is involved in teaching, by example, the necessity of humility and servanthood. (John 13:12-17)

C. **In love, serve one another** – ministry in the church

1. The Greek word for serve, δουλεύω (douleuo), means "To be a slave to; be in bondage, (do) serve (-ice)."

2. Servanthood in the local church demonstrates love for one another. (Galatians 5:13)

3. Servanthood in the local church creates unity that the body needs. (1 Corinthians 1:10)

D. Make me a servant – ministry in the world. We have been called to go with love and humility and serve our world.

1. Love, grace, and faith require that the servant find his place in God's plan. (Ephesians 2:8-10)

2. The wonder of abundant life must be shared in order to be fully experienced and appreciated. (Luke 9:24)

3. The servant will never be fulfilled or fulfill his ultimate purpose apart from the miracle of servanthood. His generation needs him serving in his area of ministry, in his unique way. (1 Peter 4:10)

4. The world will never understand the mission of Christ apart from the unity of God's servants. (John 17:23)

Notes

Study Questions – Essential Seven

1. What is the Seventh Essential of Spiritual Maturity?

   _____

   _____

   _____

2. What is the confession that believers can make after being grounded in the Seventh Essential?

   _____

   _____

   _____

3. What are the three levels of the church's work?

   _____

   _____

   _____

4. Define the three levels of the church's work.

   _____

   _____

   _____

5. What are the five keys to being used of God in His vineyard?

   _____

   _____

   _____

   _____

6. What is the ultimate call of Christian commitment?

_____

_____
_____

the Worship Center

The Center Of It All...

CHRISTIAN CHURCH

9553 Parkway East
Birmingham, AL 35215
www.theworshipcentercc.org

Printed in the United States
116979LV00001B/1-186/A